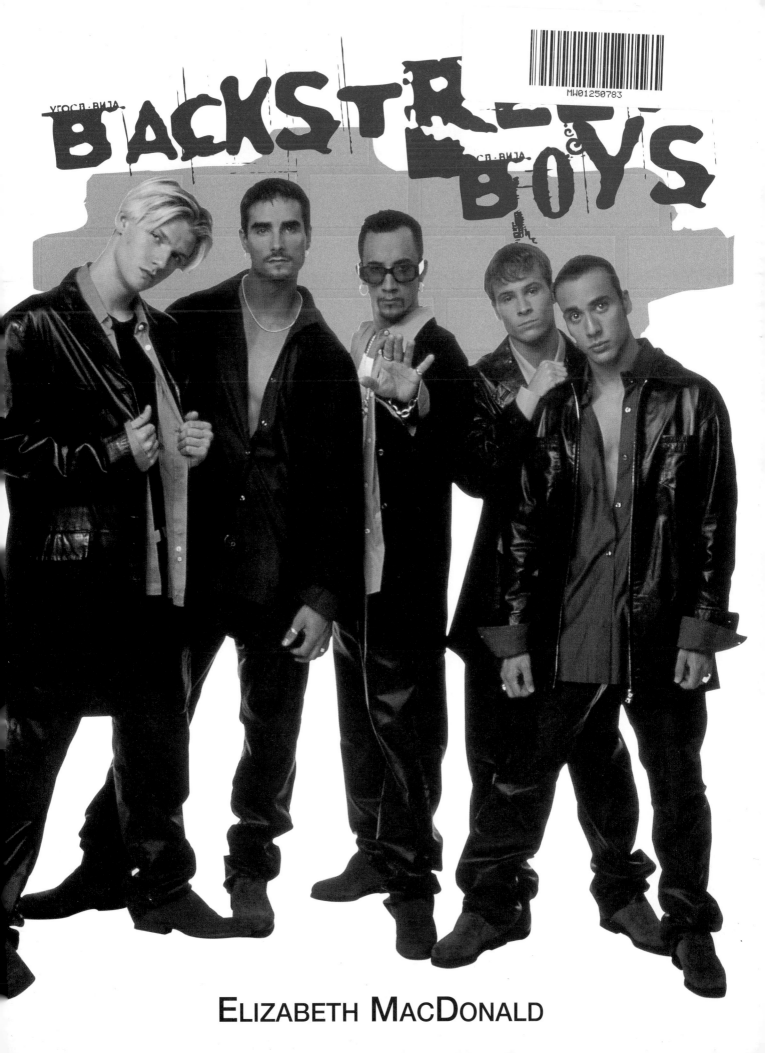

BACKSTREET BOYS

ELIZABETH MACDONALD

THIS IS A CARLTON BOOK

Copyright © 2000 Carlton Books Limited

This edition published by Carlton Books Limited 2000
20 Mortimer Street
London
W1N 7RD

The publishers would like to thank the following sources for their kind permission to reproduce the pictures in this book:

All Action/Justin Thomas 5tl, 36, 39/Suzan Moore 7tl, 29br/Doug Peters 16, 40t, 47br
Famous/Casper 9br, 34r /KurtKrieger 19b/S. Pessina 20b, 29cl/Hubert Boesl 20t, 28br, 48/Per Houby 26b
London Features International 3/Ilpo Musto 17, 26t/Ron Wolfson 21t, 28cl/George DeSota 37br/David Fischer 47tc
PA News/EPA 4, 38, 42, 46tr/KIPA Press 32
Pictorial Press 6tl, 8tr, 18, 22, 27, 43
Retna/David Atlas 47tl /Wilberto vd Boogaard/Sunshine44/Larry Busacca 1, 5br, 21b/Bill Davila 19t, 24/25, 29tr, 46bl /Steve Granitz 2/Roslyn Gaunt 6br, 7br, 8bl, 9tl, 15t, 35/B.Khan 40b, 41/Larry Miller 23/Melanie Edwards 33, 34bl/John Spellman 45
Rex 30/31/Brian Rasic 14

All rights reserved.

Printed in Great Britain by Butler & Tanner, Frome, Somerset

A CIP catalogue for this book is available from the British Library.

ISBN 1 84222 174 4

Art Editor: Adam Wright
Design: Michael Spender
Picture research: Catherine Costelloe
Production: Garry Lewis

CARLTON
BOOKS

CONTENTS

INTRODUCTION

Backstreet Boys are a group who need no introductions. Growing out of the theme park entertainment circuit in Orlando, Florida, and going on to become highly respected international pop superstars, AJ, Nick, Kevin, Brian, and Howie worked tirelessly for a number of years to break markets across the globe, giving up their personal lives, privacy, and time off to earn every bit of their success.

It took a long time for the group to be accepted in the US—perhaps the country was not ready for another boy band, following so soon as Backstreet Boys did in the wake of New Kids on the Block. But, undeterred, the Boys took themselves off around the world a few times, scored number ones all over the globe, and grew ever more confident, until the time came when they felt the US was ready to see what they could do. Even at that stage, they were considered to be little more than teen-fan fodder in a lot of circles; the group's life expectancy was around three years, at which point it was thought the band would be exhausted, outdated, and running out of ideas. In fact the opposite happened. The Boys decided to take control of the multimillion-dollar business which is their band, and at the same time made sure they were given adequate time off to rest, touch down on reality and write songs. They took a step back and started leading the way when it came to image and musical direction. Others began to follow and the ideas and inspiration kept on coming.

Sales records have been smashed, awards won and charts topped all over the world, and Backstreet Boys have finally been recognized as more then just a boy band. Now in their eighth year, on the brink of unleashing their fourth, much-talked about album onto the world, and despite one marriage, one engagement and five burgeoning solo careers, Backstreet Boys really are still Larger Than Life.

HERE'S THE STORY SO FAR...

NICK

FULL NAME: Nicholas Gene Carter
BORN: January 28 1980, Jamestown NY
STAR SIGN: Aquarius
HEIGHT: 6′ 1″ **EYES:** Blue
NICKNAME: Nick
HOBBIES: Nintendo, drawing.
FAVE FOOD: Pizza
FAVE DRINK: Coca Cola
FAVE TV SHOW: *Beavis and Butthead*
FAVE STAR: Sigourney Weaver
FAVE MUSICIAN: Michael Jackson
BEST BUYS: Sneakers and gold jewelry

IDEAL GIRL: One with brown hair and a good personality
PREVIOUS JOBS: Lead in school production of *Phantom Of The Opera* and roles in commercials for the Florida Lottery.

The youngest, joint-tallest member of the BSB gang, and also the most popular with the fans, has been working in the entertainment world for almost as long as he can remember. One of his first big breaks was when he landed a role in *Phantom Of The Opera* at the age of eight. He may have been blessed with angelic, pretty-boy looks, but being the youngest in the group has its disadvantages too — until recently, the rest of the band would tease him about being the baby and wind him up with stories of their wild nights out clubbing, knowing that he was too young to join them! The Carters moved from New York State to Florida when Nick was a kid. They're a large family comprising mom Jane and dad Robert, who used to run a retirement home in Florida, and four younger siblings—BJ, Lesley (a model), and twins Angel and Aaron.

DID YOU KNOW? NICK IS A LICENSED SCUBA DIVER.

KEVIN

FULL NAME: Kevin Scott Richardson
BORN: October 3 1972, Lexington KY
STAR SIGN: Libra
HEIGHT: 6' 1"
EYES: Green
NICKNAME: Kev
HOBBIES: Basketball, playing keyboards
FAVE FOOD: Mexican
FAVE COLOR: Blue
FAVE TV SHOW: Roseanne

FAVE STAR: Tom Cruise and Nicole Kidman
FAVE MUSIC: R. Kelly, Prince, Teddy Riley, and Babyface.
FAVE MOVIE: *Top Gun* and the *Shawshank Redemption*
IDEAL GIRL: One who accepts him as he is
FAVE PIECE OF ADVICE:
"If you can dream it, you can do it."

The oldest and most serious member of the group, Kevin had an idyllic childhood, spending the first nine years of his life on his family's farm in Kentucky. He got his first keyboard in his freshman year of high school and spent his teens entering talent contests, hanging out at his drama club and singing with a choir as well as sharing a musical ambition with his cousin Brian. Kevin comes from a close, supportive family consisting of two older brothers, Jerald and Tim, and his mom, Ann, who's a sales clerk. His father Jerald, who tragically died of cancer at the age of 49, was the one who encouraged Kevin to move to Orlando and pursue a career in music. Once Kevin arrived in Orlando, it was to be a long wait before fame and fortune would come his way, but he filled in his time with odd jobs at Walt Disney World, dressing up as Aladdin and a Ninja Turtle to entertain the crowds! Those days must be a distant memory for superstar Kevin who is now known by his bandmates as Train, because once he gets going there's no stopping him!

DID YOU KNOW? KEVIN IS A QUALIFIED BALLROOM DANCE INSTRUCTOR.

ALEXANDER JAMES MCLEAN

AJ

FULL NAME: Alexander James McLean
BORN: January 9 1978,
West Palm Beach, Florida
STAR SIGN: Capricorn
HEIGHT: 5' 9"
EYES: Brown
NICKNAME: AJ
HOBBIES: Swimming, shopping,
writing poetry, and dancing
FAVE FOOD: McDonald's

FAVE DRINK: Mountain Dew
FAVE TV SHOW: *Seinfeld*
FAVE STAR: Dustin Hoffman, Geena Davis
FAVE MOVIE: *Pulp Fiction*
FAVE SMELL: Joop! for Men
IDEAL GIRL:
One with nice eyes and long hair
PREVIOUS JOBS:
Dopey in Snow White

Only-child AJ's an old hand in the entertainment industry, having enjoyed a successful career since the age of six. By sixth grade, he'd performed in 27 shows, including the *Nutcracker* and *Fiddler On The Roof*, and when he was in junior high he landed a contract with Nickelodeon and became a regular face on TV. AJ's mum Denise has always been very supportive of her son and for a long time would join the Boys on the road, acting as tour manager. She and AJ have been very close since his dad, Bob, left when AJ was just four. Never losing sight of his ambition to be a huge star, between kids' TV appearances AJ attended auditions constantly. It was at one of those auditions that he met two of his future bandmates, Howie and Nick, and had to leave school early when he landed the BSB job. These days AJ is known as the most flamboyant of the boys. He's had more hairstyles than he's had hot dinners and seems to have so many tattoos that he looks like he's in danger of running out of space for any more (actually he has eight, but that's more than most people!)

DID YOU KNOW?
AJ IS A PUPPETEER.

BRIAN

FULL NAME: Brian Thomas Littrel

BORN: February 20 1975, Lexington, KY

STAR SIGN: Pisces

HEIGHT: 5' 8"

EYES: Blue

NICKNAME: B-Rok

HOBBIES: Basketball, weights, listening to music

FAVE FOOD: Macaroni cheese

FAVE DRINK: Iced tea

FAVE MOVIE: *Star Wars*

FAVE STAR: Sandra Bullock

FAVE MUSIC: Boyz II Men

FAVE SMELL: Safari

IDEAL GIRL: One with nice eyes and her own career

FAVE PIECE OF ADVICE: Never give away a secret

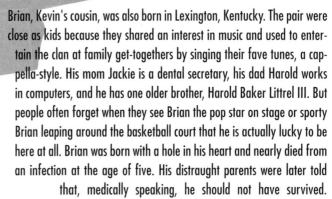

Brian, Kevin's cousin, was also born in Lexington, Kentucky. The pair were close as kids because they shared an interest in music and used to entertain the clan at family get-togethers by singing their fave tunes, a cappella-style. His mom Jackie is a dental secretary, his dad Harold works in computers, and he has one older brother, Harold Baker Littrel III. But people often forget when they see Brian the pop star on stage or sporty Brian leaping around the basketball court that he is actually lucky to be here at all. Brian was born with a hole in his heart and nearly died from an infection at the age of five. His distraught parents were later told that, medically speaking, he should not have survived. Determined to live life to the full after his narrow escape, Brian jumped at the chance of the Backstreet Boys audition that his cousin Kevin had called to tell him about while he was in a history class at school. He's still loving every minute of it.

DID YOU KNOW? BRIAN IS AFRAID OF HEIGHTS.

HOWIE

FULL NAME: Howie Dwayne Dorough
BORN: August 22 1973, Orlando, Florida
STAR SIGN: Leo
HEIGHT: 5' 6" **EYES:** Brown
NICKNAME: Howie D
HOBBIES:
Water skiing and going to the movies
FAVE FOOD: Chinese/Asian
FAVE DRINK: Sprite
FAVE MOVIE: *Outsiders*
FAVE STAR: Tom Hanks

FAVE MUSIC: Bobby Brown
FAVE COLOR: Purple
IDEAL GIRL:
One who is positive and supportive
PREVIOUS JOBS:
A commercial for Disney World
and small roles in
Cop and a Half and
Parenthood

Latino Howie first demonstrated his musical talents at the age of three when he performed a rendition of "Baby Face" on his grandmother's bed to the accompaniment of a tiny plastic guitar! Howie is the only band member to have been born and raised in Orlando and comes from a large family—mom Paula, dad Hope, a retired police officer, two older sisters, Pollyanna and Angela. (his other sister Caroline sadly died in 1998), and one older brother, John. It was Pollyanna who first got Howie seriously interested in a career in music. She is also a talented singer who sounds like a cross between Mariah Carey and Gloria Estefan. She remains close to her little brother and these days the two of them work together on musical projects separate from the band, notably a single that was released in order to raise funds for the Caroline Dorough-Cochran Lupus Memorial Foundation, which Howie set up in memory of his sister.

DID YOU KNOW?
HOWIE IS HALF-PUERTO RICAN
AND HALF-IRISH AND
SPEAKS FLUENT SPANISH.

WE'VE GOT IT GOIN' ON

THE EARLY DAYS...

So how exactly did these five guys with endless ambitions and tons of talent wind up getting together in the first place? Was it simply fate that brought them together in the sunny holiday resort of Orlando, one of the entertainment centers of the East Coast?

Some say it was—AJ, Howie, and Nick were all living in the area, working in and around the Disney and MGM attractions that form the nucleus of the city and attending all sorts of auditions and castings for work at these major studios. AJ and Howie happened to share the same singing teacher, who changed the course of pop history by introducing his two students to each other. They clicked instantly and would regularly meet up and attend auditions together. That's when they got chatting to a young, blond, cute-looking surfer type called Nick Carter who was attending all the same auditions too. The three lads began

whiling away the hours waiting for their names to be called by singing Temptations songs together a cappella. As you can imagine the results were pretty impressive and the trio soon began to gain a reputation in entertainment circles as "Those three guys who sing harmonies all the time."

Meanwhile, Kevin had grown bored of singing in a local Top 40 covers band back home in Kentucky and had packed his bags and headed for Orlando to seek success on a bigger scale. First stop was a job as a tour guide at Disney World, followed by parts as Aladdin and a Ninja Turtle. It wasn't too much fun wearing those costumes in the blazing heat of Florida, but it paid the rent and it also meant Kev had tons of free time to work on his singing and songwriting. It wasn't long before one of his new friends heard his singing voice and was so impressed that he suggested Kevin meet up with another group of guys he knew who sang mean harmonies. Guess who? You've got it—Kevin hooked up with AJ, Nick, and Howie, and they agreed that Kevin's voice fitted in so well with their style that he just had to join their group.

It wasn't long before an ad in the local paper—New record company seeks talent for new boy band—caught the boys' eyes. The ad had been placed by Lou Pearlman, cousin of Art Garfunkel (one half of Seventies duo Simon and Garfunkel) and music-obsessed local businessman, who had decided to set up his own record company, track down the best talent in Orlando and turn his protégés into a supergroup to rival Eighties phenomenon New Kids on the Block. Pearlman was inundated with applications from local pop hopefuls but he narrowed them down to the best 50 and held auditions at his mansion in June 1992.

> ## AJ WAS THE FIRST TO BE TOLD HE HAD A PLACE—HE WAS JUST FOURTEEN AT THE TIME

Four of the boys who turned up to the audition totally blew Lou Pearlman away. He knew he'd find some talented kids but these guys surpassed even his expectations. AJ was the first to be told he had a place—he was just fourteen at the time, but Pearlman was impressed by his dance moves and wacky personality. Next was Howie, who had years of acting and singing experience under his belt to back up his obvious talent. Nick Carter was selected next; at just twelve years old he already had star quality as well as an amazing voice and good looks. Then there was Kevin, who had both the looks and the songwriting skills of a potential star.

But everyone agreed that a fifth member was needed to complete the line-up. No one suitable had been found though the auditions, but Kevin had an idea—he called up his cousin Brian, whom he knew shared his love of music and, more importantly, was in possession of a fantastic singing voice that Kevin just knew would fit in perfectly with the sound his new band was trying to create. Brian will never forget the day he was sat in a history class and heard his name being announced over the school tannoy system. At first he thought he must have done something wrong, or that it was bad news, but when he got to the phone and heard his cousin's excited voice telling him to get himself down to Orlando as soon as he could, he realized that this was a once-in-a-lifetime chance, boarded a plane, and arrived in Orlando the very next day. Of course, his voice worked like magic with the other four. Brian signed on the dotted line and Backstreet Boys was born.

They had the talent, the ambition and the backing; all they needed now was a name. The boys wanted something that summed up what they were doing, but also one that said something about where they came from. At the time there was a busy flea market in Orlando called the Backstreet Market, which became a big empty parking lot when the market was closed. All the local kids would hang out there, socialize, and listen to loud music. The boys thought this was kind of cool, so they borrowed the word "Backstreet" and added "Boys" because, as they explained, "No matter how old we get, we will always be boys!" The flea market itself is no longer there—a new complex has been built on the site, but thanks to these five lads it will live forever in the minds of pop fans all over the world.

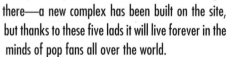

The first thing the five new band members had to do was get to know each other, both musically and personally. They all got on well, but it would be a while before they started to feel like one big family. They started rehearsing hard in Lou Pearlman's warehouse in Kissimmee, singing covers of current chart songs by groups such as Boyz II Men, as well as classics by artists such as Smokey Robinson. They also played live as often as possible, mostly in and around Florida, knowing their act was more than good enough and trusting that the right person from a big record company would eventually spot them and sign them up. This was also a good way of getting used to playing live together as a group. Their first single, "Tell Me That I'm Dreaming," came out on Lou Pearlman's own independent record label and just a few hundred copies were put onto tapes, which were given out to their new-found fans and to record companies. Their next step was to get a big support slot and while they were waiting for that to happen the boys used the time to perfect their act by touring schools and colleges.

All five Backstreet Boys were determined that their group would stand out from the rest. They refused to be thought of as just another bunch of pretty faces, so they made sure they sang live and had as much input into the creative process as possible, organizing their own dance routines and stage costumes. And eventually it paid off—at long last they were noticed and started getting bookings to support huge acts like En Vogue and Brandy when they came to play in the Orlando area.

This amount of exposure could only lead to one thing—a record deal. First the group were signed to Mercury Records, but were heartbroken to be dropped soon afterwards when it was felt that the musical climate in the US at the time was such that a new boy band was just not going to be accepted. But their disappointment didn't last long— they were snapped up straight away by Jive Records, home of one of their idols, R Kelly. And then the hard work really started. With the extra money the record deal brought in, the group were able to hire a team of top choreographers, stylists, voice coaches, and producers who could add the professional touch that would help push Backstreet Boys right to the top.

HEY, MR DJ
(KEEP PLAYIN' THIS SONG)

FIRST STEPS TO STARDOM...

At last Backstreet Boys were ready to record their first single for Jive. The aptly-named "We've Got It Goin' On" was recorded in Stockholm, Sweden with the help of hit-master Denniz PoP and released at the same time in the United States and Europe. In those days the music scene here in the States was still very grunge-orientated and the music-buying public just weren't ready to accept what looked like just another boy band. The single only reached number 69 in the Hot 100. However, in the UK the single fared much better. The British pop press were blown away by the song and it got rave reviews everywhere, radio stations loved it and added it to their playlists and the group were booked to appear on all the big British music shows, including *Top Of The Pops*.

The Boys' second single, "I'll Never Break Your Heart," did even better in the UK charts. Although it failed to dent the Top 20, the group was becoming well-known and success in other countries, including Germany, Austria, and Canada quickly followed. In February 1996, 3,000 screaming Canadian fans turned up to see the group perform live at a shopping mall in Montreal before their single was even released there. Six months later, when Backstreet Boys returned to the city to perform at a festival, their audience had grown to 65,000 people! No one could believe it—especially not the band members themselves, but it was only a taste of things to come.

The group had decided to forget about trying to make it in the States for a while and to concentrate on their loyal fans in Europe and Canada, hoping that American fans would eventually come around to their way of thinking. The whole of Canada and Europe were now waiting for their favorite group to release their first album, knowing that it was going to be a classic. They weren't wrong. *Backstreet Boys* was released in April 1996, at the same time as their third single, "Get Down (You're The One For Me)," and both releases helped establish the band as one of the biggest names of the decade.

In the summer of 1996, the group hit the road on their first ever headline tour, bringing their Backstreet magic to 57 venues throughout Europe and the United Kingdom. Not surprisingly, every show was a sell-out and when "We've Got It Goin' On" was re-released at the end of the tour, the tired but jubilant boys held a blowout party in a posh London club to celebrate. They must have known the single was going to go through the roof this time—it did, reaching a very respectable number 3 in the UK charts.

Asia was the next continent to fall under the Backstreet spell. The group's debut album flew out of the shops when it was released there in September 1996 and the group wasted no time in hot-footing it across the water to give their Asian fans a taste of what they could do live. Their sell-out tour took in countries such as Hong Kong, Korea, Japan, and Malaysia. Around this time they also visited Singapore, the Philippines, Australia, and New Zealand. The fivesome didn't see their own beds for months!

Meanwhile, awards were coming in thick and fast, the best of the bunch being the Select Award at the MTV Europe Awards in November 1996—the equivalent to the MTV Viewers Choice Award in the States. No wonder a couple of the boys were in tears when they won—they'd beaten off The Spice Girls, who at the time were MASSIVE. Soon after this they set off on another huge European tour, released their fourth smash hit single, "Quit Playing Games (With My Heart)," which zoomed up the charts all over Europe, and released "Anywhere for You," a special Valentine's Day single with personalized messages to their fans. Then they began to prepare for their planned tour of Canada.

In Canada, Backstreet mania had reached even crazier heights than it had in the UK, especially in Montreal. Poor AJ had to abandon all hope of performing dance moves for a few nights of the tour because his leg was in plaster—a huge gang of fans in the city had accidentally crushed his foot as he tried to get past them! Devoted fans bought up every last one of the tickets for BSB's Montreal show in just half an hour! Seventy thousand people saw the boys perform live on their Canadian tour and by April 1997 their debut album had gone six-times platinum, meaning it had sold 600,000 copies! Their second album, *Backstreet's Back*, was released in Europe in September 1997 and the boys celebrated in true BSB style. A fancy satellite link-up meant that the boys, who were in New York, were able to speak to press all over Europe about their latest release.

It had always been just a matter of time before fans in the USA caught onto the fact that we were missing out on something big. The Boys had sold millions of copies of their album worldwide, played to huge crowds in countries they never thought they'd even visit, and had fans going mad, fainting and screaming wherever they went. Everywhere except at home. At first they didn't mind—in fact they quite enjoyed visiting Orlando and Kentucky on their rare weeks off and being able to wander about with their friends and families without being mobbed as they were everywhere else on the planet. But in the fall of 1997, Nick told *Tiger Beat* "We're ready to show everyone out there what we've got." And they were. They knew it was going to be tough, as they'd seen first-hand how much work has to be done to make it big in any country, but Backstreet Boys also had invaluable experience and the confidence that comes with success and stardom. Their debut US single, "Quit Playing Games," reached number 2 in the Hot 100 in June 1997. The album *Backstreet Boys* (a variation on the album of the same name released elsewhere), which the group finally released in the States in August 1997, reached number 12 in the US album charts. The boys were ecstatic.

"THAT" VIDEO

One particular single and its accompanying video stands out more than any other in the story of Backstreet Boys. The anthemic "Everybody (Backstreet's Back)" was a real turning-point for the group; it proved to their doubters that this was no run-of-the-mill boy band and that Backstreet Boys were a lot stronger, more powerful, and imaginative than a lot of people thought. It also propelled the group into the pop stratosphere with more force than the Boys ever could have hoped. "Quit Playing Games" had broken the US market and Backstreet Boys were safe in the knowledge that their follow-up single was arguably, even better. "Everybody..." had a thumping dance rhythm and would become the nearest thing the group had to a theme tune. All they needed was a top-class video to go with it. And they had an idea about that. They'd all remembered how powerful Michael Jackson's spooky *Thriller* video had been back in the Eighties and had always wanted to make something similar—a Backstreet version for the Nineties. And now the success (and money) was rolling in, they realized they were in a position to undertake this huge project. So, in June 1997 the group headed for a disused aircraft hangar on the outskirts of LA where a team of top make-up artists sat each Backstreet Boy down and spent hours transforming him into a menacing ghoul. Brian became a werewolf, Nick, a mummy, Howie turned into Count Dracula, Kevin was Dr Jekyll and Mr Hyde, and AJ became the Phantom of the Opera. The results were incredible and director Joseph Kahn, the Boys, the make-up artists, and a bunch of dancers and extras—with a lot of help from the set designers who built the creepy castle—worked for three days straight to make this phenomenal short movie about pop stars in a house of horror.

"MILLENNIUM SOLD A RECORD-BREAKING 1.1 MILLION COPIES IN ITS FIRST WEEK OF RELEASE"

The next couple of years were a juggling act for the group, trying to spend plenty of time touring and promoting in the European and Asian countries where they had long been successful, while keeping things going with their new fans in the States too. Exclusive interviews became a rare occurrence because the band only had a limited time to cover TV appearances, radio interviews, live shows, and magazine interviews on each stop along their way. Journalists would complain about being given just ten minutes to interview the whole band and take pictures for a cover story, while radio interview times would also be cut right back. They may have been spreading themselves thinly, but Backstreet Boys had no choice—after all that's just what you have to do when you're one of the biggest bands in the world. What really mattered was that despite the fact that they were exhausted, missing their friends and families and had had their privacy snatched away from them, Backstreet Boys were still putting out brilliant singles, and performing live with more style and professionalism than ever.

Another milestone for the group came on May 18, 1999, with the worldwide release of their third album, *Millennium*. It was highly acclaimed and sold a record-breaking 1.1 million copies in its first week of release. Since then it has gone more than twelve times platinum, spending more than 45 weeks in *Billboard*'s Top 200 album chart (mostly in the top ten). The album was honored with no less than five, count 'em, Grammy nominations including one for Album of the Year. You might expect the boys to have rewarded themselves with a bit of time off, but no—since the release of the album, Backstreet Boys have been relentlessly promoting *Millennium*, writing material for their next album and have set more records with their sell-out 42-city European tour and two more sell-out US tours, including a date at the huge 70,000-seater Atlanta Dome.

THE ONE

There's one big drawback to being a member of a hugely successful group like Backstreet Boys—you don't get much time for romantic relationships. A date or two could just about be fitted around the group's punishing schedule, but with the demands of touring and promoting, not just in the US but in every corner of the globe—as well as recording and rehearsing—long-term relationships were out of the question, especially in the early days when BSB really were working 24/7.

The irony is that wherever Backstreet Boys went there were thousands of adoring female fans who'd have done anything to go on a date with their fave band member. Much as the boys appreciated this, the chances were that they hadn't even had time to go home and visit their families in the last few months, let alone take a lucky girl on a night out. They weren't complaining, of course, but the life of a top pop star can be lonely in a lot of ways.

In the past year or so, since Backstreet Boys have become mega-stars and some of the pressure to work 24 hours a day is off, they've finally been able to relax a little, take a small step back and find time to do those normal things they have missed out on. Two of them have even settled down into serious relationships...

LOVE FILE: AJ

AJ McLean is the biggest flirt and most romantic member in the group. He puts this down to being brought up in an all-female household and always getting on better with the girls at school than with the other boys, who thought he was a weirdy! If he likes someone at a party, he'll walk past her a few times until he feels ready to say "Hi." Then he'll keep her chatting and entertain her with lively stories. If he really likes her, he might even hit her with some romantic poetry! His first crush was on one of his teachers, Mrs Olney—he remembers trying to be good in her class, but he didn't really mind when she gave him detention because that meant he could have her undivided attention! Then he dated a girl called Jennifer for two years. He did have a girlfriend called Marissa back home for a while and he was really upset when they had to break up due to his busy schedule, but he still considers her to be a good friend. She even came with him on tour once or twice. Out of all the Backstreet Boys, AJ is the one who revels in the attentions of the fans and is most likely to scribble down their numbers and surprise them with a phone call. He has lots of female friends and at the moment his priority is having fun, but he has managed to maintain a long-term relationship with his girlfriend Amanda Latona, a singer and dancer.

LOVE FILE: KEVIN

Although Kevin is the oldest he is also the shyest member of the group when it comes to chatting up girls. If he liked a girl he'd talk to her about subjects he was interested in, such as music or travel, not necessarily letting on that he liked her. It would take a while for Kevin to feel comfortable enough with a girl to talk about more personal topics. In fact, his on-off long-term girlfriend Kristin Willits, now his wife, was the first girl he had ever chatted up! He'd met Kristin before the band had even started, back in the days when he was dressing up as a Ninja Turtle at Walt Disney World. She was working there too—as a dancer on Beauty and the Beast. It was obviously love at first sight when they met in the Disney staff cafeteria because it's not Kevin's style to go and chat up a stranger at all. But it paid off and the two dated for six months before Kristin went off to work on a cruise ship and Kevin got caught up in Backstreet fever. From then on, it was long-distance love. "We ended up breaking up for a while," he remembers. "It was hard."

Many of Kevin's friends back home began to settle down and start families while he was away from home, putting all his energies into the group. And for a while he was desperate to have a long-term relationship himself, but it was impossible—the group were never in one place longer then a couple of days. Happily, when the Boys' schedule began to cool off just a little, the couple were able to start seeing more of each other again. In November 1999, at a BSB concert, Kevin grabbed a quiet moment with Kristin's father and asked for her hand in marriage. Just before Christmas of the same year, he drove Kristin to the beach near Orlando where he had first told her he loved her, and gave her a beautiful engagement ring. The pair wed in a private ceremony on June 17, 2000, with the other four Backstreet Boys all in attendance.

LOVE FILE: BRIAN

Brian's another one who is extremely unlikely to go up to a girl and chat her up, but while he would be flattered if a girl came up to him, he would play a little hard to get while he worked out whether he really liked her! He is attracted to girls who are out-going and independent—like his fiancée Leighanne Wallace, five years his senior. The couple met on the set of the "As Long As You Love Me" video in 1997, on which actress Leighanne was an extra, and have been continuing their long-distance relationship ever since, meeting up whenever they get the chance. Brian has been quoted as saying that both knew this was "it" when they first met—awww! And Leighanne has stuck by Brian through good times and bad—she's seen the group rise from unknowns in this country, to one of the biggest bands there is, and has been right behind him all the way. She was also a major support to Brian when he underwent heart surgery in 1998. "She was the second face I saw when I woke up from the operation," he recalls. The co-writer of "Larger Than Life" proposed to Leighanne—who unsurprisingly said "yes" straight away (who wouldn't!)—on Christmas night 1999 and the couple celebrated over the millennium. Fans at recent BSB concerts have shown that they were happy for the couple, although some jokingly hold up signs reading "Marry Me Instead!"

LOVE FILE: NICK

Nick has a girlfriend called Mandy, although it is a bit of an on-off affair thanks to—you've guessed it—the band's workload. When Nick first started off in the group he was very young and hadn't had much experience with girls. He soon began to get huge amounts of attention from female fans and really didn't know what to do. But he soon got used to it! The problem came when he met someone in a one-to-one situation that he really liked, because he'd get a tingly feeling in his stomach and become too shy to talk to her!

But he's grown up a lot since then and the rest of the group now agree that Nick is the second most romantic Backstreet Boy, after AJ. He finds all the attention "very flattering" and has been quoted as saying that he is very happy that fans feel they can relate to him. He doesn't mind what a girl looks like because for him, it's what's inside that counts. A good heart and a good personality are top of his list and he also finds self-confidence attractive. When he does meet someone special he spoils them and showers them with gifts—lucky lady!

But before Nick gets to that stage he has to get talking to his girl. If he were to see someone he liked, he'd make eye contact by looking at her until she looked back at him and if she held his gaze, then he'd go over and talk to her and pay her compliments about her eyes or hair. When they'd chatted for a bit longer and he'd decided he was really smitten, he might send her some roses the next day. All in all, honesty is the most important quality in any relationship with Nick, so anyone who's going to mess him around or who only likes him because he's a Backstreet Boy need not apply. He also finds smoking a big turn-off.

LOVE FILE: HOWIE

The last remaining totally single Backstreet Boy Howie usually goes for a romantic approach when he meets a girl he likes. There are two sides to Howie's character—the sweet side and the red-hot Latin lover side! He has been known to serenade a girl with a song (a bit like a personal BSB concert!) or say something complimentary to her in Spanish, his second language.

Howie D started dating when he was 14, when he asked out a girl he was in a play with, and the young lovers were driven out on their first date in her mom's car! Howie's never been shy of the ladies, but he takes his love life very seriously, never giving too much away. Although he is romantic enough to know exactly what to say to get a girl's heart racing, he never says anything he doesn't mean; he has too much respect for that. Sincerity is the key with Howie—he would never dream of two-timing. He's had a couple of serious relationships since hitting the heights of fame with Backstreet Boys, but neither of these worked out—blame the band's hectic schedule. He was heartbroken both times, but ever the professional, the band always came first.

Howie's ideal date would have a sense of humor and a sparkle in her eyes. She would also be self-confident, spontaneous and very affectionate, as Howie likes nothing better than to be given a big hug. Lookswise, he's not really bothered as long as his girl is happy with herself and doesn't hide under layers of make-up, baggy clothes and fake fingernails! Other big no-nos are arrogance and not getting on with his family.

ANYWHERE FOR YOU

LIFE ON THE ROAD WITH BACKSTREET BOYS...

A big part of the life of a Backstreet Boy is touring, and the Boys are certainly used to life on the road by now. It means being in each other's company 24/7 which can get a little hairy sometimes, but they still show respect for each other and have a lot of laughs together. In fact, they're closer than ever and know each other about as well as any five guys can do...

One of the most interesting things about traveling the world is sampling all the different cultures and getting taste for the weird and wonderful food native to each. The boys have extra-big appetites when they're on the road thanks to all that energetic dancing and they make sure their tour bus and hotel fridges are overflowing with their fave food. AJ's so glad that there's a branch of the golden arches in nearly every city in the world now because he eats McDonald's wherever he goes, but the others just hate the way he never shares his fries! He thought the food in England was the worst he had ever eaten and stuck to McD's the entire time he was there. Brian and Nick are into potato chips, candy bars, and KFC while Howie and Kevin are much more health-conscious and insist on supplies of fruit, veg, and other healthy stuff being available wherever they go. Howie and Kevin are also the most adventurous when it comes to trying local food when they're in a foreign country—Howie loved the fish and chips he tried when he was in London and he also tried some authentic Indian food in the English capital while he was there. Kevin samples all sorts of different foods, but he admits that after a long time on the road he starts missing his mom's home-cooked chilli!

AJ is the biggest party animal of the band. "I'm the one who persuades everyone else to party when we're on tour. I'm out of control. I think people would be really shocked to know what we're like!" he once confessed. Sometimes he gets the other guys to join him on one of his crazy nights out during tours, but he's definitely the leader when it comes to partying hard. He has even been known to stay out clubbing so late that the band have missed their plane the following morning!

> "I'M THE ONE WHO PERSUADES EVERYONE ELSE TO PARTY WHEN WE'RE ON TOUR. I'M OUT OF CONTROL. I THINK PEOPLE WOULD BE REALLY SHOCKED TO KNOW WHAT WE'RE LIKE!"

Being the eldest, Kevin relates really well to the Backstreet band that accompanies the group on tour "They're experienced musicians in their late twenties and thirties and have amazing stories to tell. I love good company," he once revealed in an interview. Kevin can often be found staying up late in the hotel bar, swapping tales of the rock'n'roll life on the road with the Backstreet band and crew.

Nick has his Gameboy in his pocket at all times when traveling and if he's not playing on that he'll plug in his headphones and listen to some of his favorite music or get one of the hairdressers to sort out his hair. Sometimes he'll amuse everyone by drawing cartoons

of the other guys! If the group are driving somewhere, Brian enjoys literally watching the world go by through the window. AJ might mess around playing jokes on the others, or kick back with his headphones on and try to block out everything that's going on in the outside world. All the guys love basketball and insist on taking a hoop with them whenever they go on tour. They can always be seen fooling around with the ball backstage and on their rare days off. On one of their first European tours they played a charity basketball match against their rivals 'NSync in front of a crowd of 18,000 in Germany. Not much chance of that happening now the two groups are arch-enemies! (Oh, Backstreet Boys' team won easily, of course!)

Nick's hotel room is always a tip, although he still hasn't reached AJ standards of messiness—AJ's room is always ankle-deep in food wrappers! But in the early days of doing back-to-back shows, the Boys didn't have a hotel at all and used to sleep on their plush tour bus complete with a jacuzzi and two lounges, and had to compete with each other for the best bunk beds. Nick used to get onto the bus first to bag the best spot—somewhere near the back—but he hated trying to get a night's sleep on the move because it was cold and he was sometimes kept awake by Howie snoring! He also accused Howie of talking in his sleep, although he usually couldn't understand what he was saying.

It was on the Boys' second European tour that they realized just how many fans they had and were forced to up their security for their own protection and for the protection of their fans. A free open-air concert in the Spanish capital Madrid was canceled during 1997 because so many fans turned up that there were worries some of them would have been crushed. Everywhere the boys go, there are thousands of fans waiting to pounce on them. All very flattering, of course, but it becomes frightening when you can't leave your hotel room without a security guard to lead you through the crowds. Obsessed fans began somehow finding out the Boy's schedule in advance and checking themselves into the hotels that they knew their idols would be staying in, splitting the cost between six or more, making full use of the hotel's internal phones, and wandering the corridors in search of any sign of the Boys. A year or so after BSB started, while they were away touring Europe or Asia, their families back home began to find themselves on the receiving end of phone calls and visits from strangers at all times of the day and night. The more popular the group became,

the more fans traveled to the homes of their idols to see exactly where the Boys grew up, and in the end poor Mr and Mrs Carter had to put up an iron fence around their house to protect their family!

One two-hour concert, let alone a two-hour concert every night of the week, takes an awful lot of stamina and the boys have to be sure to keep their vocal chords in tip-top condition. They sing a cappella together for at least thirty minutes before each show and then sing some more just before they go on. One thing that really helps is keeping their vocal chords moist by drinking gallons of herbal tea with honey and lemon. Howie finds this especially helpful. Nick prefers to put his voice through its paces by singing a few scales pre-show, while Brian finds that the opposite—giving his voice a break—works best for him. AJ does all he can to avoid catching colds, including—unfortunately—not kissing too many fans. Kevin's trick is to stay away from dairy products such as milk and cheese, because they produce a lot of mucus in his throat (yuck!) which does his singing voice no favors at all.

You're in the auditorium, the lights have gone down and you're waiting for Backstreet Boys to come on. So what's the hold-up? What exactly are they doing backstage? Well, strong religious beliefs have always been a big factor in gluing this group together and an example of their faith can be seen in their pre-show ritual. While you're holding your breath waiting for them to come on stage, the five band members are in the dressing room, huddled in a group, and holding hands with key members of their entourage. Someone is chosen to say a prayer out loud—an unrehearsed, spontaneous speech, thanking God on behalf of every-one for their good luck and good health. Anyone else in the dressing room stays silent until they hear the boys say "Amen." BSB then give each other a final good-luck hug before following a security guard, who leads the way through the darkness with a torch, to take up their final positions on stage. This ritual, which they have performed before every single concert since 1993, keeps them grounded, helps them to remember where they came from, and to be grateful for all they have achieved.

AS LONG AS YOU LOVE ME

THE BOYS ON EACH OTHER...

When you consider how much time these guys have spent with each other it's amazing that they still get on so brilliantly. OK, so they're all branching out a bit these days and working on projects separate from the band, but so would you if you'd spent the past eight years with the same group of friends-stroke-workmates!

The secret of the band members' ongoing friendships can be put down to lots of things, but most importantly it comes down to respect for each other. AJ, Howie, Nick, Brian, and Kevin confide in each other, have fun together and treat each other like members of a family, always being sure to give one another the space they need. Sometimes they fall out with each other—that's only natural—but when this happens, instead of allowing tempers and resentment to simmer under the surface, these guys will make sure they talk about what's bugging them. Even if it means a big bust up (which does happen occasionally) the Boys make up straight away, give one another a hug and forgetting about the problem as soon as they can. Of course, each of the boys has his own annoying habits—they wouldn't be human if they didn't, would they?

KEVIN

Strong, silent Kevin is the one whom the rest of the Boys go to when they need advice. After all, he's the oldest and has a lot of life-experience. But on the other hand he can also be a bit mysterious, keeping himself to himself. He takes his work very seriously, and makes sure he is always totally on-the-ball when it comes to the business side of things. But he's not miserable, as some people think—he's just a perfectionist who waits for the right time and the right place before he lets the lighter side of his character shine through. The rest of the boys have learned to keep out of his way when things aren't going right 'cos Kev has been known to be a bit moody. In the early days of the group, Kevin and Nick wouldn't see eye to eye with each other a lot of the time, but the older Nick gets, the better the two of them get on. Kevin's a lot happier these days since he got together with Kristin and spends every spare minute with her.

BRIAN

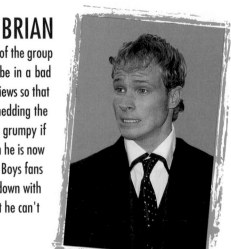

Joker of the pack B-Rok just can't help acting the funny guy pretty much all of the time. The rest of the group usually find him hilarious, but he can get a little annoying if the boys are tired or happen to be in a bad mood. But Brian does have a serious side to his character, and he tries to put this across in interviews so that fans realize he has feelings as well as a talent for making people laugh—he even admits to shedding the odd tear when BSB have won a big award or scored a number 1 single. He also gets extremely grumpy if he hasn't had enough sleep or is feeling particularly homesick. Brian used to be much shyer than he is now and the whole group agrees that the success of the band and the adoration of all the Backstreet Boys fans around the world have really brought him out of his shell. Since he met Leighanne and settled down with her Brian has become even more relaxed and at ease with himself. He often feels frustrated that he can't spend more time with his fiancée but, luckily for Backstreet fans, he always puts work first.

AJ

Chatterbox AJ McLean just doesn't know when to be quiet and he often has to be told when he's getting on the rest of the band's nerves. He doesn't mind when that happens—he just whips out his cell phone and calls someone back home instead! Probably the least shy of all the Backstreet gang, AJ is always fooling around doing some crazy thing or other—as much to amuse himself as anyone else. The rest of the guys tease him constantly about his habit of hogging the limelight, but that's just the way AJ is. He might be a good talker, but he's also a good listener and the other band members know they can turn to him if there's something they need to talk over. The only problem is that AJ finds it a little hard to keep secrets and has been known to blurt out information that was meant to be for his ears only! Like most people, AJ also has a deeper side to his character, which has earned him a reputation for being the intellectual of the group as well as the crazy party animal. One of his fave pastimes is writing poetry, which has been known to inspire him to pen lyrics too. When he's not writing poetry, AJ will often read a serious literary masterpiece by Shakespeare or TS Eliot.

NICK

It's hard to believe now, but up until a couple of years ago when he turned 18, Nick still had to be chaperoned everywhere he went and was being tutored while on the road. Nick has changed and grown up a lot since the band started and the age gap between him and, say, Kevin, the eldest, is much less obvious. Kevin used to find Nick's inability to concentrate on anything infuriating, and had to pull himself up and remember that Nick was just acting like any regular teen. In a lot of ways Nick's been lucky as he's been able to look to the older member of the group for guidance and advice. In the early days especially, Brian took Nick under his wing and the two would be the closest in the group, earning themselves the nicknames Frick & Frack because they were so inseparable. The rest of the guys all agree that Nick is clumsy and, at times, hyperactive. Like any normal young man he has an apparently endless supply of energy, which is a much-needed quality when you consider the schedule that these boys have been on for a long time now. Nick also has the ability not to let things get to him, which the others envy and find frustrating in equal measures. As for being the most popular band member with female fans, Nick finds it flattering but at the same time he says he can't see what all the fuss is about. The rest of the guys don't mind—they knew from the start that one of them would attract more attention than the others and after all it's not as if they don't have a share of the adulation themselves...

HOWIE

Every successful group needs a member like Howie—a peacemaker who stays calm when the going gets tough and can see every side of an argument. If the group has a disagreement or a discussion, Howie will listen to everybody's point of view before he voices his own opinion. The rest of the group all agree that Howie is caring, respectful and honest—it's just the way he was brought up. Howie tries at all times to live his life by the motto "Treat others the way you would like to be treated yourself." He wouldn't dream of disrespecting or lashing out at anyone and he hopes he is generous, fair, and honest at all times. Which isn't to say that he's over-earnest or boring—far from it. Howie is second only to AJ as the partying king of the group. He likes nothing better than to go out to a club and do the moves on the dancefloor. Howie's always up for a laugh and doesn't take himself too seriously—he couldn't really with the other guys constantly ribbing him about his unruly hair and his offbeat dress sense.

NO ONE ELSE COMES CLOSE

HEAD TO HEAD WITH THEIR RIVALS 'NSYNC...

While Backstreet Boys were breaking the European and Asian pop markets back in 1996, there was a new boy band from Orlando called 'NSync following hot on their heels. 'NSync—JC, Joey, Lance, Justin, and Chris—sang harmony-led pop and were determined to to become the biggest group in the world. (Sounds familiar?) They'd formed the group themselves, and had approached Lou Pearlman to ask if he would represent them after hearing about the success he'd had with Backstreet Boys. After securing Pearlman's backing, 'NSync set about making it in the same way as Backstreet Boys had the year before—targeting Europe and Asia before heading home to the States to conquer the market here.

Comparisons between the two
groups were inevitable. There were five members in each combo,
they were American (there weren't that many boy bands coming out of the States at the time) and
most of all, 'NSync's hard-edged but harmonious pop sounded just that little bit too familiar for BSB fans' liking. That their agent Lou Pearlman had started representing another boy-group had put BSB's noses out of joint but Backstreet Boys ignored their competitors, considering them to be nothing more than a second-rate copycat group who might be pinching some of their ideas, but who'd never be able to steal their fans.

But the problems began when 'NSync started making it big in the States around 1998 with releases such as "Tearin' Up My Heart," while BSB were still torn between the US market and busying themselves wooing the crowds in Europe and Asia. It didn't seem right that Backstreet Boys had worked so hard to pave the way for boy bands to be accepted again by American audiences and then, while their backs were turned, another sound-a-like group should stroll right up that path and begun selling records by the bucketload.

Then, in fall 1999, 'NSync did something that BSB never thought they would. They broke off their contract with BMG records, sacked Lou Pearlman and announced that they were moving to BSB's relatively small label Jive! AJ, Nick, Kevin, Brian, and Howie were gobsmacked. They'd always considered Jive to be like a family to them—after all, they'd looked after them from the start and had felt as if they were all "in it together" on their small label. Now they had signed 'NSync, their biggest rivals, it felt almost as if Jive had lined up a replacement.

The rivalry grew even more intense when 'NSync released their (admittedly impressive) album *No Strings Attached* in March 2000. The album title and the sleeve of the CD, on which the group was shown with strings hanging off their limbs like puppets—a comment on the fact that they would not be told what to do by any record company—only served to annoy the BSB camp even further. And what was even harder to swallow was the fact that *No Strings...* outsold *Millennium* and smashed sales records, selling 2.4 million copies in its first week of release, whereas *Millennium* had sold 1.1 million. The unthinkable had happened and war was declared. In an interview AJ announced that it will be "Bye, bye, bye" to 'NSync when BSB's next album is released at the end of 2000, because it will blow *No Strings...* out of the water. There's no doubt in any BSB fan's mind about who is the more talented group and BSB's forthcoming album was always going to be great—now it's got to be the best ever. Hey, a little bit of healthy competition never did anyone any harm, did it?

QUIT PLAYING GAMES

TOO MUCH FUN...!

Of course, it's not all work, work, work being a Backstreet Boy—as you can imagine, with a pair of jokers like Brian and AJ in the group, there's a lot of fun to be had too.

Brian is particularly good at winding up the rest of the group and is such an uncannily talented impersonator. Nothing lightens up the atmosphere backstage better than a spot of mickey-taking and luckily all the boys are able to join in and laugh at themselves when they are the butt of a joke. Nick is often on the receiving end because the rest of the guys think it's funny that he's the most popular with the fans. They amuse themselves by making Nick go first when they are trying to leave a venue or hotel that is besieged by fans so that he gets mobbed and the rest of them can sneak past while Nick is getting the brunt of all the attention! Once AJ, Brian, Kevin,

and Howie took this a bit far, shoving Nick out of the dressing room into a crowd of waiting fans while he was wearing nothing more than his underwear! Needless to say, the fans couldn't believe their luck... Nick took his revenge by sneaking into AJ's hotel room and stealing all AJ's clothes, causing Mr Fashion to freak when he woke in the morning and realized half his beloved wardrobe had gone missing.

The crew that travel with the Boys on tour—the lighting techs, roadies, and sound people—also enjoy a good laugh at the Boys' expense. Before a soundcheck at a huge venue they once replaced all the microphones on stage with carrots, turned down the lights and waited to see the Boys' expressions when they came on stage and started singing!

Some of the awards that they have won have often caused the Boys to chuckle. Most recently Kevin was voted the 'Sexiest Pop Star' by *People Magazine*. The rest of the group still haven't stopped ribbing him about it—he's become known in band circles as "Mr Sexy!" Kevin came in for even more stick when soon afterwards a European magazine crowned him "Mr Body Beautiful." It might have caused Kevin's bandmates to fall off their chairs laughing, but you'll probably agree that he was very deserving of the title.

> " ONCE AJ, BRIAN, KEVIN, AND HOWIE TOOK THIS A BIT FAR, SHOVING NICK OUT OF THE DRESSING ROOM INTO A CROWD OF WAITING FANS WHILE HE WAS WEARING NOTHING MORE THAN HIS UNDERWEAR! "

Some of the laughs come from accidents that happen while the boys are on stage. One time, AJ was hit in the crotch by a sun-glasses-wearing banana that had been thrown by a fan in the audience and admits that he was laughing so hard that he couldn't sing for a while! Another time Nick threw his arms out during a dance-move and knocked poor Howie right off the stage! That wasn't the only time Howie landed up where he shouldn't have been—he once rolled so close to the edge of the stage that a security guard had to grab his T-shirt to stop him falling into the pit far below. And AJ still cringes when he recalls the time that halfway through a concert, his jacket got caught in the percussionist's drumkit and he knocked the whole thing right over! Not the sort of thing he really wanted to happen, especially in front of thousands of fans. But he had to laugh—after all, the rest of the band (and the audience) thought it was hysterical.

LARGER THAN LIFE

THE BOYS AND THEIR IMAGE

Clothes and image are an important factor in the success of any band and Backstreet Boys are no exception. In the early days of the group when they were just getting started, their image was carefully controlled by their record company and the Boys were encouraged to wear co-ordinating outfits to help present an image to the world that said "We are together as a group." It wasn't that the Boys minded this, but as five guys with unique tastes in clothes it got a bit boring and they decided they would prefer to express their individual styles more. And of course, the more successful the band became the more freedom they had to do this. They still have stylists to get hold of outfits for video shoots and live concerts, but these days BSB are totally in control of what they wear. If they don't like something, they won't wear it—simple as that. And why should they when they have such great taste themselves...?

AJ has always had the most outlandish and individual taste in clothes. Even at school he stood out from the crowd, wearing ghetto-style clothes one day and the preppie look the next. He would even borrow his mom's clip-on earrings sometimes and wear them in class, a memory that still makes him laugh. His weird and wonderful dress sense went down a treat with the girls in his class, but the sporty boys at school just thought he was downright strange. Now he's a big-time pop star, AJ is able to give free rein to his creative way with clothes—he is rarely seen without his shades (he has so many pairs he has lost count), he has eight tattoos (and counting), loves experimenting with his facial hair, and he has changed his hairstyle more times than he can remember. AJ adores thinking up elaborate ideas for video shoots—well he would, wouldn't he, they're another excuse for dressing up!

NICK'S style is pretty down-to-earth. Let's face it, he would look good in a garbage sack, so he doesn't really have to try too hard. His blond hair is one aspect of his appearance that does tend to change from month to month—for ages it was long and floppy, then it gradually got shorter and he is currently wearing it mussed-up with white-blond highlights. Nick says he aims for an image that is as normal as possible so that fans can relate to him—anything classic with a sporty or preppie twist and Nick is happy.

KEVIN has always been Mr Classy when it comes to clothes, reflecting his serious and mature personality. He digs designer labels, but nothing too showy, and he is often seen wearing all black. During his time off he likes wearing football shirts and jeans, but for dates, interviews, and TV appearances, he goes for the smart option every time, which suits him down to the ground. His hair has barely changed since the early days of the group although at one point he grew it longer and would often be seen in a black beanie hat.

BRIAN'S thing is jewelry. He owns all manner of diamond-encrusted pendants, rings, bracelets, and earrings which he swaps around to contrast with whatever clothes he's wearing. He's another one who can look good in anything from a smart suit to a football shirt. Brian wears his light-brown hair short and lets it curl naturally at the front, lightening it up with a few blond highlights.

HOWIE D could never be called a fashion victim. Not because he doesn't know what the latest trends are, but because he dreads looking the same as everyone else. Howie notices what's in fashion and wears the opposite, a policy that works and means that he always stays one step ahead of the pack. Howie spent years fretting about his curly Latin hair that he couldn't keep under control and that meant every day was a bad hair day for him. He even got his mom to relax his hair in his junior year, which was a bad mistake—all his classmates thought he was wearing a toupee! Bad hair days are a thing of the past now for Howie, who's grown his hair long enough to slick back into a bunch, so he can forget all about it.

SHOW ME THE MEANING OF BEING LONELY

HOW THE BOYS COPED
WHEN FACED WITH TRAGEDY...

More than any other band of our time, Backstreet Boys' lives have been dogged by tragedy and illness. Not only have the Boys had to deal with the pressures of growing up in the spotlight, the lack of privacy that being a celebrity brings and the sleepless nights that are an inevitable by-product of touring the world—they have also had to cope publicly with the illness and deaths of several close friends and members of their families.

Nor have they escaped illness themselves—Brian Littrel himself underwent serious heart surgery in May 1998. Unknown to the thousands of fans who were enjoying BSB's 1998 European tour, Brian was harboring worries about his health. He had been born with a hole in the heart and at five years old had nearly died after contracting a blood infection. Although, mercifully, he survived, he still had to have regular hospital check-ups to make sure everything was OK. One of these routine checks was fitted in around the Boys' unbelievably heavy schedule early in 1998, when they had been working nonstop for months. Brian's specialist noticed

"HOWIE WASTED NO TIME IN SETTING UP A FOUNDATION IN HIS SISTER'S NAME—THE CAROLINE DOROUGH-COCHRAN LUPUS MEMORIAL FOUNDATION "

that the singer's condition had worsened—probably aggravated by over-work—and Brian was told that an operation was necessary to sort out the problem. He could carry on and finish the tour, but he would have to go under the surgeon's knife as soon as it was over. Needless to say, Brian was extremely worried about the prospect of another visit to hospital—he still had bad memories of the last time he stayed in one as a five-year-old boy—but he faced his ordeal with maturity and faith in God.

The timing of Brian's operation couldn't have been worse—the night he went into hospital, Backstreet Boys had been booked to play their most important show to date—in their hometown at Walt Disney's Magic Kingdom—a homecoming gig of epic proportions. Many tears were shed backstage that night—not just tears of gratitude that Backstreet Boys had come home heroes, but tears of sadness and sympathy for their brother who was missing what would have been one of the greatest nights of his life.

A day later, while they were still on a high from their fantastically well-received show, Nick, AJ, Howie, and AJ heard the news that they had all been waiting for—Brian's operation had been a complete success and he was expected to make full recovery. "Get Well" cards poured in from fans and helped Brian along the road to full fitness.

But that was not the last of the traumas the boys would face. Later that year, while they were in the middle of touring the US, Howie heard that his 37-year-old sister Caroline Dorough-Cochran had died. She had been suffering from the skin disease lupus for some time, but her death came as a big shock and Howie and the rest of the Dorough family were naturally devastated. Howie flew straight home to be with his parents, remaining sisters, and brother Johnny, and the final three dates of the BSB US tour were post-poned as a mark of respect to Caroline. Not being one to sit back and let things happen without taking control, Howie wasted no time in setting up a foundation in his sister's name—The Caroline Dorough-Cochran Lupus Memorial Foundation, which raises money for research into the disease. Howie has since said that his sister's death has made him "be the strong one in the family—the one that goes out there and makes a difference."

The foundation has raised thousands of dollars through releases such as an EP featuring Howie and his sister Pollyanna singing a duet—"Fly To Heaven"—and events such as the benefit concert Lupus 2000, which took place in Orlando on June 25, 2000, raised over $100,000 for the charity.

There was yet another shock to come for Backstreet Boys in 1998, which turned out to be both the group's best and worst year. Denniz PoP, the Stockholm-based pop-mastermind behind the group's first single, "We've Got It Goin' On," and their most recent at the time, "Show Me The Meaning Of Being Lonely," died of stomach cancer. All the boys were devastated to lose not only a great producer, but someone who had become a mentor and good friend to them over the years. At around the same time Kevin and Brian lost their beloved grandfather to the same disease.

Kevin already knew only too well what it feels like when someone close to you dies—he had lost his father to cancer in 1991. He pointed out later, "it was ironic that 1998 was probably the most successful [year] of our lives, but there was an awful lot of heart-break going on under the surface that BSB fans didn't necessarily know about at the time." It certainly was a rollercoaster ride of a year, not helped by the fact that there were all sorts of legal and financial wrangles going on at the same time between the band and their management company.

However, the Boys have come out the other side stronger as people and stronger and more supportive of each other as a group. The video for their recent single, "Show Me The Meaning Of Being Lonely," was inspired by these people that the Boys had loved and lost and couldn't have been more serious—it even depicts Brian having heart surgery. "We wanted to show that life as a member of one of the world's biggest pop groups is not all glamor," explains Brian. "Everybody has to deal with tragedies and loss."

MILLENNIUM

WHAT DOES THE FUTURE HOLD FOR BACKSTREET BOYS?

A lot has happened in the eight years since Backstreet Boys got together as a group. Their music has reached out to people in every corner of the globe—Europe, Asia, and Australasia as well as the US. Their third album, *Millennium*, broke sales records when it was released in 1999 and also became the first recent teen-pop album to be acclaimed by critics and taken seriously by adult audiences. The single "I Want It That Way" even spent 52 weeks on *Billboard*'s Adult Contemporary Chart. They are also six-times Grammy nominees (if you count both the 1999 and 2000 ceremonies), which is no small achievement in itself. So how have the Boys changed and grown, and what are their plans for the future?

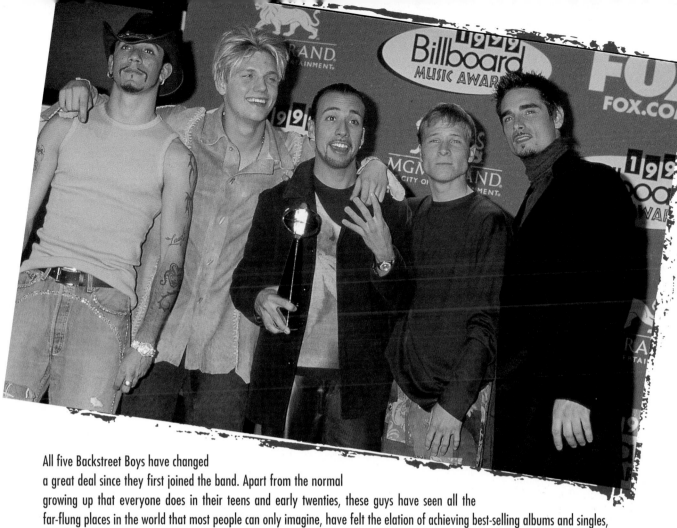

All five Backstreet Boys have changed
a great deal since they first joined the band. Apart from the normal
growing up that everyone does in their teens and early twenties, these guys have seen all the
far-flung places in the world that most people can only imagine, have felt the elation of achieving best-selling albums and singles,
adulation from fans everywhere, and sell-out tours, as well as the devastation of losing people close to them. All this against a back-
drop of exhaustion, stress, and constant exposure in the media. It's enough to make anyone grow up pretty quickly. They also had
to learn rapidly about the business side of the music industry in order to be able to take control of their finances and careers when
they realized in 1998 that certain people behind the scenes would like to force the group down the traditional boy band three-
years-then-burn-out-and-split route. This was never an option for a group like Backstreet Boys, who are now in a position to con-
tribute self-penned and self-produced tracks to their much-anticipated forthcoming album, and who show no signs of winding down
despite the fact that their achievements are beyond most bands' wildest dreams.

So apart from the new album, what's next on the cards
for Backstreet Boys? Brian still has a wedding to plan for,
of course, but neither this nor Kevin's marriage is expected to affect the band as a whole. As AJ put it, "It did come
as a surprise when we heard Brian was engaged, but I
knew Kevin was going to do it for a long time. We're all
growing up and it has to happen to everyone sooner or
later. As long as everyone in the group is happy with what
they're doing in their private lives then everything's cool.
We'd only speak up if someone was doing something that
would have a negative effect on the band." Kevin has
been spending every free moment with his wife
Kristin—after all, being with the love of his life is something that he has dreamed about for quite some time
now. When he's not hanging out with his fiancée

> "AS LONG AS EVERYONE IN
> THE GROUP IS HAPPY WITH
> WHAT THEY'RE DOING IN
> THEIR PRIVATE LIVES THEN
> EVERYTHING'S COOL"

Leighanne, or fundraising on behalf of his charity organization the Brian Littrell Healthy Heart Club For Kids, Brian has been getting big into songwriting—something that he has always enjoyed. In fact, workaholic Brian even spent almost his entire six-week break writing new material and he is expected to have a number of credits on the new BSB album. Nick is also taking the songwriting route, writing and producing material for an un-named rock band made up of friends. He will play drums on the forthcoming album, while Kevin will play the piano.

Meanwhile, Howie and AJ have both been working on solo projects—Howie mainly to help raise funds for the Caroline Dorough-Cochran Lupus Memorial Foundation—the charity that he set up in memory of his sister. A fluent Spanish speaker whose idea it was to record translations of a number of BSB tracks including "Quit Playing Games" into his second language a few years ago, Howie is also developing solo material along the lines of a Ricky Martin, Latin-type vibe. He has been writing material for other acts such as EYC and Mandy Moore as well, and has taken on a couple of minor acting roles, such as a part of an alien in WB's sci-fi drama series *Roswell*.

Typically, it is AJ who has commanded the most attention with his solo project Johnny No-Name, an alter-ego who is rapidly taking on a life of his own and whom AJ swears is more popular than the real AJ (we say "no way!"). Johnny first entered the spotlight with a mini solo tour in March 2000 to benefit the VH1 Save The Music Foundation, which helps restore music in public schools, and pleased the crowds with renditions of rawk-out tracks by Prodigy and Stone Temple Pilots. AJ/Johnny plans to record a funky-sounding album one day, and AJ says he is happy to have found a way of being himself outside Backstreet Boys. "There's a lot more freedom with Johnny," says the singer.

But these solo projects are no indication that Backstreet Boys' days are numbered. No way. AJ, Brian, Nick, Howie, and Kevin are just finding new ways to express themselves after eight years as five-fifths of a a hugely successful pop group. The reality is that the band are stronger than ever. At the time of writing, the Boys have finished another sell-out US tour and have just returned from a twelve-day songwriting trip to the Bahamas, where they penned at least eight tracks for their forthcoming album, due out late in 2000. According to AJ, the trip was hard work, but great fun. Sounds it—they spent their free time jet-skiing, scuba-diving, and gambling, all of which brought the five of them into focus as a band all over again, after a six-week post-tour break. Soundwise the album is expected to be a little more edgy, more grown-up sounding than their previous LPs. "Our tastes have become a bit more sophisticated," explains Brian. The group is aiming for a raw, natural feel to the production which sounds intentionally less polished than usual—a little bit like The Beatles. Musically it's rumored to be a mixture of rock, R&B, hip hop, and country. Can't wait to hear it...

BACKSTREET'S BACK, AGAIN, EVEN BIGGER AND BETTER THAN BEFORE.

FIFTY FASCINATING BACKSTREET FACTS

1. Howie has lost his luggage more times than any other band member

2. Nick once gave the band's manager gum that tasted of fish. Bleugh!

3. Kevin never travels without pictures of his family and fiancée in an envelope

4. Nick's mom wrote a book about her son's life, *The Heart And Soul Of Nick Carter.*

5. Howie is the tidiest in the group

6. AJ collects hats

7. In spring 2000, the group let fans choose which was to be their next release from *Millennium.* They chose "The One," by voting on MTV

8. Howie and AJ recently presented Mariah Carey with an award at the World Music Awards in Monaco—and were surprised by the smallness of Mariah's dress!

9. Howie and AJ are even bigger workaholics than the rest of the group

10. Brian was wrongly accused of shoplifting in a K-Mart superstore!

11. What Brian really wants is to get married, have a family and for BSB to go from strength to strength

12. Nick showed his ball skills early in 2000 when he played in a charity soccer match

13. Howie enjoys a visit to Sea World in Florida when he has a day off

14. The Boys recently collaborated with Lionel Ritchie on a single—"Cinderella"— but no release date has been confirmed so far

15. Nick once auctioned off his couch for charity. The only problem was that three people won and it had to be sawn into bits!

16. These days, the boys each have their own bodyguard

17. When they finished their last US tour the Boys went bowling and paint tagging to celebrate

18 Nick decided to gel his hair straight up in the cab to the Billboard Music Awards in December 1999

19. AJ reckons the most important thing he does every day is clean his teeth

20 When Brian proposed to Leighanne she was working as a dancer for Cher

21 Kevin was once engaged to a girl called Beth, but at 19, he decided he was too young and called it off

22 Kevin has a four-year-old goddaughter called Madison

23 AJ once had a job as a ventriloquist

24 AJ's voice has deepened by two octaves since he first joined the band

25 Kevin came down with appendicitis in 1995 and had to have an operation

26 Backstreet Boys once shared a dressing room with The Spice Girls in Germany, at the Girls' special request!

27 Nick sometimes gets embarrassed by the suggestive banners held up by fans at some of their concerts

28 In an auction, two Howie fans bid $15,500 each to have dinner with the star. The money went to his lupus charity

29. Brian and AJ can't stop biting their fingernails

30 When Howie first auditioned for the group his stage name was Tony Donetti, which lead to a mix up in which he nearly didn't get called back

31 Brian has a gold necklace spelling out B-Rok, which he had made in Australia

32 AJ once said that when he's rich he'll buy an English castle!

33 Nick's little brother, Aaron, once supported BSB in Berlin, Germany

34 AJ once introduced the support act dressed as The Riddler from *Batman*, because he thought the costume was cool

35 AJ won $1,000 in a talent contest when he was twelve years old... and spent it all right away!

36 When Brian was seriously ill at the age of five, his heart stopped beating for a full 20 seconds.

37 Nick has three tattoos—a musical note on his right shoulder blade, a dolphin on the top of his left arm, and a band around his right arm

38 Believe it or not, there are plans to build a Backstreet Boys theme park ride in Florida! A fitting tribute since the Boys hail from Orlando—the theme park capital of the world

39 Rival BSB and 'NSync fans faced each other in a charity basketball match in Poughkeepsie, NY.

40 Howie never wants to even see another Gummi Bear since he said in an interview that he liked them and got inundated by packets from fans. He ate the whole lot!

41 Until a couple of years ago, AJ would never go any-where without his "Blankey" a blanket knitted for him by his grandmother. He was devastated when it was thrown into the garbage by a cleaner at a hotel in South Carolina

42 Two Backstreet fans once stowed away in the luggage compartment of the Boys' tour bus!

43 Brian used to sleep on a king-size waterbed, which he bought for $50

44 Sometimes the other guys tease Brian about having a Southern accent, calling him a "bumpkin!"

45 When the Boys turned up to present an award at the 1997 Billboard Awards, they were all wearing identical sneakers

46 For a few days in 1998, Kevin worked as an underwear model in Milan. Cooor!

47 Girls at school used to laugh at Nick for wanting to be a singer

48 Kevin goes gooey every time he sees a baby

49 The engagement ring Brian bought for Leighanne is canary yellow

50 On Kevin and Kristin's wedding day, Kristin's mom said "It's great he became what he is, but we knew him when he was a Ninja Turtle!"